sports coach
UK
The National Coaching Foundation

WITHDRAWN

how to coach children in sport

ISBN 1 902523 53 9

Based on material from *Working with Children*
© The National Coaching Foundation, 1989 (ISBN 0 947850 58 9)

Author: Chris Earle
Editor: Nicola Craine
Sub-editor: Warwick Andrews
Designers: Leanne Taylor, Sandra Flintham
Cover photo courtesy of actionplus sports images
All other photos courtesy of **sports coach UK** and actionplus sports images

sports coach UK would like to thank Lyn Goodliffe
for her valuable input into this resource

Published on behalf of
sports coach UK by

sports coach UK
114 Cardigan Road
Headingley
Leeds LS6 3BJ
Tel: 0113-274 4802 Fax: 0113-275 5019
E-mail: coaching@sportscoachuk.org
Website: www.sportscoachuk.org

Patron: HRH The Princess Royal

Coachwise Solutions
Coachwise Ltd
Chelsea Close
Off Amberley Road
Armley
Leeds LS12 4HP
Tel: 0113-231 1310 Fax: 0113-231 9606
E-mail: enquiries@coachwisesolutions.co.uk
Website: www.coachwisesolutions.co.uk

Contents

actionplus

contents

Introduction

Coaching children can be a rich and satisfying experience. It is also a tremendous responsibility. As a coach, you play a vital role in the development of children's basic motor skills and their long-term attitudes to, and enthusiasm for, sport and physical activity. These developments are essential if children are to become long-term participants and achieve their potential.

Children's attitudes and approach to sport will be shaped and influenced by their experiences during your coaching sessions. Enjoyable experiences can encourage children into a lifetime of healthy, enjoyable sport and physical activity. Poorly planned and badly delivered sessions, however, may put them off sport for life.

This resource provides a basic introduction to coaching children with plenty of practical advice to help you create a positive sporting environment for the children you coach. Subjects covered include:

- the talent development process

- basic facts about the physical and mental development of children

- developing skill

- practical coaching tips

- adapting sports for children

- legal and ethical responsibilities.

As you read through the resource, keep the five golden rules of coaching children in mind:

sports coach UK

1 Adopt a child-centred approach.

2 Make it fun.

3 Involve the parents/carers.

4 Reward effort as well as achievement.

5 Develop the athlete ... then the player.

- Throughout this resource, the pronouns he, she, him, her and so on are interchangeable and intended to be inclusive of both males and females. It is important in sport, as elsewhere, that both genders have equal status and opportunities.

- In the context of this resource, the term *children* is used to refer to children and young people up to the age of 18, and vulnerable adults who may have additional needs.

- Although the emphasis of this resource is on coaching, it is aimed at all those who lead or deliver children's sports programmes (eg coaches, leaders, teachers, instructors, development officers, officials, administrators, volunteers, parents/carers) and those with responsibility for the organisation of children's sport (eg national governing bodies, local authorities, centre managers, sports clubs).

Talent development process

The success of performers at the highest level is widely acknowledged as a process that begins in childhood and which can take more than ten years to achieve. It relies on children valuing and enjoying the experience of physical activity. Coaches, teachers, sports leaders and, above all, parents/carers, have a crucial role to play in these essential early stages of development. This section focuses on three models which promote a long-term approach to developing sporting talent.

Bloom's three-stage model

Bloom's three-stage model[1] describes the essential characteristics of performers, coaches and parents/carers during the talent development process (see Table 1).

Table 1: Summary of Bloom's three-stage model

	Early years	Middle years	Later years
Performer	• Joyful • Playful • Excited	• Wider perspective • Committed • Identity linked to sport	• Obsessed • Responsible • Consumed
Coach	• Kind • Cheerful • Focused on talent development process	• Strong leader • Knowledgeable • Demanding	• Successful • Respected/feared • Emotionally bonded
Parent/ carer	• Model work ethic • Encouraging • Supportive • Positive	• Makes sacrifices • Restricts own activities • Child-centred	• Limited role • Provides financial support

3

1   For full details, refer to Bloom, BS (1985) **Developing talent in young people**. New York, Ballantine Books. ISBN 0 345319 51 6

Coaches working with children should:

- consider the characteristics within each of the three stages

- establish what the children want to get out of their involvement in sport

- consider their own approach as a coach

- recognise the important role played by parents/carers.

Cote's three-stage model

Cote's three-stage model[1] considers the influence of the family in the development of talented performers and relates to the *early*, *middle* and *late* stages of Bloom's model (see page 3). It also reinforces the need for children between the ages of 6 and 13 to have access to positive and multiple sporting experiences in order to develop into adults who are long-term, regular participants in sport and physical activity (see Table 2).

Table 2: Summary of Cote's three-stage model

Sampling years Age 6–13	Specialising years Age 13–15	Investment years Post-15
• Emphasis on fun and excitement • Parents/carers are key influence • Need to sample wide range of activities • No sport-specific specialisation	• Focus on one or two sports • Sport-specific skill development • Practice time important • Lifestyle management (balance of activities)	• Committed to achieving elite status in one sport • Massive amount of practice time • Family becomes a *sporting family* (ie family activities revolve around young person's sporting timetable)

4

---

1   For further details, refer to Cote, J (1999) **The influence of the family in the development of talent in sport**. *Sports Psychologist*. Vol 13.

Each of the three stages demands different coaching skills. Coaches may not necessarily possess all of these and may therefore consider specialising in just one of the stages. This allows children to progress from stage to stage under the guidance of different specialist coaches.

> The phrase *progression, not possession* is frequently used to describe how coaches should view their role in moving children up the performance ladder.

Long-term Athlete Development

Balyi's Long-term Athlete Development (LTAD) model[1] promotes sport as a valuable activity which is enjoyable and which contributes to a healthy lifestyle. It encourages young people to participate in sport and provides opportunities for them to improve their skills and achieve their potential. Following the four stages outlined in the table on pages 6 and 7 will help young people to achieve the three main, inter-linked outcomes of LTAD:

- Lifelong participation

- Improved performance

- Physical literacy.

sports coach UK

5

---

1   For further details, see Balyi, I (2002) **Long-term athlete development – the system and solutions**. *FHS*. Issue 14, pp 6–9.

(*FHS*, **sports coach UK**'s **(scUK's)** subscription magazine, is issued to all **scUK** members on a quarterly basis. For further details, contact **scUK** Membership Services on 0113-290 7612.)

Table 3: Summary of Balyi's LTAD model

Stage	Age	Key points
One: FUNdamentals	4–10	• Performers need to sample wide range of fun and creative activities • No sport-specific specialisation • Emphasis on development of basic motor skills, not competition • Parents/carers involved and supportive • Tasks/groups set by biological rather than chronological age
Stage	**Age**	**Key points**
Two: Training to train	10+	• Performers begin to apply basic skills and fitness to preferred activities • Performers begin to reduce number of sports/activities • Emphasis on training and practice, but element of competition introduced (eg 25% of training programme) • Emphasis on learning how to train, **not** on outcome

Stage	Age	Key points
Three: Training to compete	13–17 (girls)/ 14–18 (boys)	• Emphasis on development of sport-specific skills, techniques, tactics and game strategies • Performers generally have individualised conditioning programmes and specific performance goals • Over-training and over-competition must be avoided

Stage	Age	Key points
Four: Training to win	17+ (girls)/ 18+ (boys)	• Most performers train and compete on full-time basis • Performer's physical, technical, tactical and mental capacities fully developed • Emphasis on specific training to achieve and maintain optimum performance at key competitions

Each of the four stages of LTAD challenges coaches to place the children at the centre of all their planning, motivations and goals, and to always consider their best long-term interests. The first two stages are particularly relevant to coaching children. These focus on the development of children's general athletic skills – turning them into athletes first, then players.

Putting theory into practice

Applying the following key principles to your coaching sessions will help you make a positive contribution to the development of the children you coach in line with Bloom's, Cote's and Balyi's recommendations.

Make it fun

Although this sounds obvious, children vote with their feet. If they don't enjoy a coaching session, it is highly unlikely they will want to return, and they may even discourage other children from attending too. Successful coaching sessions for children involve laughter, enjoyment, excitement and fun.

- Children get bored very easily. Plan your coaching sessions carefully and provide stimulating and varied activities which challenge their creative thinking and problem-solving skills.

- Pick up ideas from other people (eg books, other coaches).

- Don't be afraid of devising your own activities – the smile (or not!) on children's faces will tell you whether or not you have succeeded.

- Remember what works and use it again, but avoid over-use as this soon becomes boring and routine.

Include several sports

Specialising in just one sport from an early age does not produce elite performers, nor does it encourage long-term participation into adulthood. In fact, it can have a negative effect and lead to burnout and under-achievement.

Allow children to experience a wide range of sports and physical activities, even if you consider yourself to be a sport-specific coach. However, remember to explain your reasons for doing so to the children and, more importantly, to their parents/carers, who will no doubt want to know why their children are playing basketball when they have paid good money for you to turn them into the next big thing in the tennis world!

By sampling a variety of sports, children are less likely to get bored and more likely to find one (or more) that they enjoy the most and want to continue playing. Many world-class performers are skilled in several sports. Lleyton Hewitt, for example, was an extremely proficient Australian Rules player before choosing tennis as his preferred sport.

- Skills learnt in one sport can often be used in others:
  - Catching and dodging skills in tag rugby can easily be transferred to basketball and other invasion games.
  - Learning to run properly in athletics is a core skill of most other games and sports.
  - The hand-eye coordination required to strike a tennis ball applies to a range of stick and ball games such as cricket, hockey, badminton, rounders and squash.
- Tactics and strategies (however simple) can also be transferred from one sport to another. For example, the triangle of three players working together in football can be used in most invasion games, as can the basic principles of attack and defence.

9

Involve parents/carers

Parents/carers play a key role in encouraging their children to take part in sport and physical activity. Although there is always a great deal of criticism of over-enthusiastic parents/carers who shout abuse and behave badly on the sidelines, those who don't encourage and support their children's involvement in sport are a much greater hindrance to long-term participation.

Children whose parents/carers actively encourage and support their involvement in sport are more likely to value and enjoy it. Parents/carers don't have to be active in the sport themselves, but they do need to recognise the benefits of, and support, their children's involvement.

It's important to communicate with the parents/carers of the children you coach:

- Explain (verbally or in writing):
  - what your coaching sessions will involve
  - what you hope to achieve
  - when and where sessions will take place
  - what costs will be involved (eg kit, transport, session fees). Apart from time, this is the biggest contribution parents/carers will make to their child's involvement in sport and they will want to make sure they are getting value for money.

- Make an effort to speak to parents/carers before and after coaching sessions. Answer their questions and make them feel part of their child's experience.

- Encourage parents/carers to get involved in your coaching sessions (eg assisting you, providing transport, supplying refreshments). Watching you may even inspire them to become coaches themselves.

Develop basic motor skills

Whatever the sport, participants need to develop as athletes first. Basic motor skills, such as running, jumping, throwing and catching, are best learned between the ages of five and twelve. Skills acquired at this stage provide a sound base for continued involvement in sport or other forms of recreation, which in turn provide positive health and social skill benefits.

- Even if you consider yourself to be a sport-specific coach, concentrate on developing children's basic motor skills. Find ways of introducing them in every coaching session, either during the warm-up, main activity or cool-down.

- Improve your own coaching methods for generic skills such as running, throwing and catching.

Put children first

Working with children is a great responsibility. Failure to provide quality coaching may put a child off sport for life or, even worse, inflict permanent damage on them.

- Be aware of how much training and competition children are involved in.

- Be aware of potential and actual injuries, and take positive action to prevent both.

- Be aware of children's fitness levels and capacity.

- Ensure that the training to competition ratio is appropriate.

- Be aware of your own limits – don't try to teach general or sport-specific activities/skills that you don't understand and cannot deliver safely.

The rest of this resource provides more detailed, practical advice on how to incorporate these key principles into your coaching practice.

Physical development

No one needs to be told that children grow, and often at an alarming speed. To coach them effectively it is important to understand how they grow and what happens during the twenty years or so it takes to finish the process.

At birth, a baby is about a quarter of its adult height. The fastest growth takes place in early childhood, up to the age of six or seven. A second growth spurt during adolescence gradually slows down until the child reaches his or her full height.

More startling, perhaps, are the changes in proportion (see Figure 1).

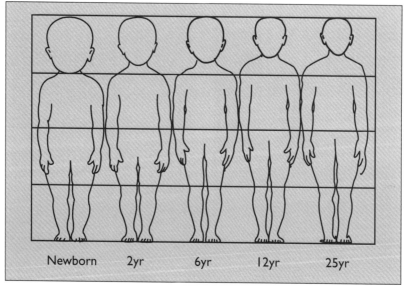

Figure 1: Changes in proportion at various ages[1]

1   Adapted from Lowry, GH (1973) **Growth and development of children**. Chicago, Year Book Medical Publishers (by kind permission of Elsevier Science).

A baby's head accounts for a quarter of its height; an adult's head accounts for only a sixth. Similarly, a baby's legs make up a third of its height, while an adult's make up half. Young children have relatively large heads (which affects their balance) and relatively short legs (which affects their running ability).

Just before the adolescent growth spurt, children's arms and legs are disproportionately long, which often make them clumsy and uncoordinated – although in some cases, long legs may give children an advantage in certain sports such as running events.

Don't judge by age alone

Muscle strength is closely related to the size of the muscles, so small children are disproportionately weaker than older children. Strength increases with age, but muscle development also depends on the child's physical maturity and children of the same age can be as much as four years apart in their physical development. This difference can be emphasised further in sports which use a fixed date to divide participants into age groups for competition. In extreme cases this can have the effect of adding another year of difference if the child's birthday is very close to the arbitrary qualifying date.

13

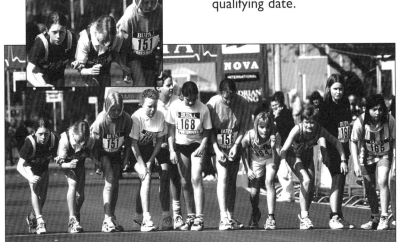

Maturity can also be affected by body shape. Broadly speaking there are three physical types: thin, muscular and fat. Children who are fat or muscular tend to be taller and heavier than their peers, but stop growing earlier, developing into shorter, heavily built adults. Thin children often take longer to mature, growing into taller, slimmer adults who may have proportionally longer legs. Children who mature early often have a greater proportion of fat in their bodies than those who mature more slowly.

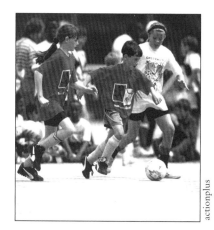

actionplus

In sport, successful boys tend to be early maturers with a muscular build; successful girls are often late developers with a thin build. Obviously, then, successful girls and boys will tend to be at very different stages of growth and development.

sports coach UK

14

Younger girls and boys can play alongside one another quite happily, but after puberty boys will be bulkier and stronger, so they should not be involved with girls in any sport where this would give them an unfair advantage. Group children according to their physical development, using height and weight as a yardstick.

At puberty

In boys, adolescence brings sharp increases in height and weight, a broadening of the shoulders, and heavier muscle development. On average the growth spurt reaches a peak around the age of 14, though it can start as early as 12 or as late as 15. Boys normally reach their adult height around the age of 17 or 18.

In girls, adolescence brings the height increase first, with the weight increase lagging about six months behind. Much of this weight will be fat. Physical changes normally include a broadening of the hips which tends to change running action. For girls, the growth spurt reaches its peak much earlier – on average at around the age of 12 though it may come as early as 10 or as late as 14. By the age of 15, girls will normally have reached full adult height.

Proportions of fat and lean tissue in the body change throughout the growth process. Both sexes use up fat in that initial surge of growth during early childhood. From then on, the proportion of fat increases steadily, though less so in boys, who may actually reduce their fat level during puberty. This gives them a greater proportion of bone and muscle, so their bodies pack more weight to the cubic centimetre than girls.

The sexual development which occurs at this time can bring physical difficulties for adolescent children, as well as causing them mental and emotional preoccupation. You will need to be particularly understanding with girls when menstruation is beginning – this may inhibit their participation in sport.

15

Puberty can sometimes have a marked effect on performance. In gymnastics, for example, girls may find that their performance deteriorates, while boys may find just the opposite.

Early and late development can cause emotional problems too. Late developers may feel they're being left behind, especially if they get teased by the others, while early developers may have problems later when the rest catch up and they find they're no longer in the lead. You should be aware of these possibilities and make sure that all children are treated with respect whatever stage they have reached.

actionplus

Practical tips

- Think about growth stages, not just ages.

- Think how changes in physical proportion will affect performance.

- Help children understand these changes and come to terms with them.

- Group children according to physical development, using height and weight as a yardstick. Carry out regular weight and height checks – even something as simple as marking names, heights and dates on a changing room wall to check for growth spurts. Avoid matching children with very different development levels, especially in contact sports.

- Encourage skill learning for everyone – slow starters could be very successful later.

Children and exercise

As children start to exercise, their need for energy grows. To supply that need, oxygen supply to the blood must rise, and blood supply to the muscles must improve. However, children don't breathe as efficiently as adults. This means young children must work much harder than adolescents or adults to provide the oxygen their muscles need.

Building the energy powerhouse

The body has three energy systems:

- Phosphagen system

- Anaerobic glycolytic system

- Aerobic energy system.

The phosphagen and anaerobic glycolytic systems produce energy for fairly short periods of time; the aerobic system can produce energy for much longer periods.

Before adolescence, children get a higher proportion of their energy from the aerobic system. However, they don't produce it as efficiently as adults. Up to around the age of ten, boys and girls produce roughly equal amounts of aerobic power. During puberty all children become more efficient in their use of aerobic power, but girls stop improving after about 14, while boys who mature more slowly can continue improving up to about 18. After puberty, boys typically have a higher aerobic capacity.

In general, young children are better at steady, extended exercises. Physical changes during and after puberty will improve their anaerobic power, and the degree of this improvement will decide, for instance, what distance is best for a child who has already shown ability as a runner.

Where next?

For further information about energy systems, refer to **sports coach UK**'s resources[1] *Physiology and Performance* and *The Body in Action.*

---

1   Available from **Coachwise 1st4sport** (tel 0113-201 5555 or visit www.1st4sport.com).

Build strength safely

Strength gains occur mainly during puberty. Children of all ages can benefit from general training and exercise. However, specific strength or weight training must not be given before bone development is complete (usually at about the age of 17) as this can cause serious physical damage. The resistance of the child's own body is quite enough to promote strength, and endurance can be developed with repeated light exercises such as circuits. As children develop, they will do better in power activities such as sprinting, jumping and throwing. Even so, strength gains may lag and you must be careful not to overload growing bones. Training intensity should be reduced during the growth spurt at puberty.

It is vital that you know and understand good exercise techniques, and that you are able to explain them clearly. This is the only way to ensure safety and the maximum possible benefit for the children.

Where next?

The **sports coach UK** resource *The Body in Action* provides a good variety of basic exercises[1].

How much can children take?

Children don't tolerate exercise as well as adults and are much less aware of their real limits. They may feel ready for more after a very short rest but you will do better to stop them before they exhaust themselves. Because children breathe more quickly than adults, they lose water more quickly too, so you should make sure that they drink plenty. As their bodies are much smaller, they are more sensitive to heat and cold. Make allowances for these things. Adequate sleep is important too – late nights and early mornings can soon reduce a child's resistance to fatigue.

18

---

1   Available from **Coachwise 1st4sport** (tel 0113-201 5555 or visit www.1st4sport.com).

Practical tips

- Never use weights before bone development is complete (at about the age of 17).

- Don't expect girls to develop much more aerobic power after puberty.

- Steady, low-intensity exercises are normally most appropriate for children. Don't use adult training programmes before puberty.

- Reduce training intensity during the growth spurt.

- Remember to include warm-up and cool-down every time.

- Watch for signs of distress. Never push children to extremes.

- Make sure children gain enough rest. Make sure they have some complete rest days. Encourage them to go to bed early.

- In cold weather, make sure children wear enough to keep warm.

- Make sure children drink plenty of fluids. This is particularly important in warm weather, when water should be available before, during and after the activity.

Developing skill

The human nerve and muscle systems only reach full maturity in early adulthood. Immaturity of development makes it harder to learn specific skills, so younger children usually have limited skills. This is not just a matter of coordination – they are less able to concentrate and make decisions.

Even so, fundamental skills learned at this time, such as throwing and catching, are the foundation for learning more sophisticated skills later on. Skill teaching is vital, but it must be done at the children's own level and when they are ready to learn – motivated, not just physically ready. If children don't want to learn, are uninterested or bored, they will simply not improve. You must therefore make activities varied and enjoyable.

Also remember that children learn a great deal by copying others – their friends, teachers, parents/carers and coaches. Imitation is powerful, so as a coach it is important for you to provide appropriate models that are technically and ethically sound.

Children often make very rapid progress. They tend to have more confidence than adults and are more willing to try new skills and less afraid of failing. (But do give the less confident ones the encouragement they need.)

The way children acquire skills follows basically the same pattern as for adults. Your role in helping them is different at each stage (see Figure 2 on page 21).

actionplus

Stage 1: Understanding

- Never assume children know what you want – show them and explain in simple terms.

- Be patient – you may need to explain what you want several times in different ways that they can understand.

- Children have a limited attention span – treat them as individuals and assess what each needs to concentrate on.

Stage 2: Practising

- Make sure your coaching sessions are meaningful and enjoyable.

- Provide an appropriate type and amount of practice.

- Communicate effectively and provide regular feedback, especially when working with children with shorter attention spans.

- Think about how best to reinforce the progress children are making.

- Make sure children have mastered the relevant skill(s) fairly well before you expect them to perform, particularly in dynamic team games.

- Make practice fun, interesting, varied and as close to the actual performance without the pressure of competition.

- Adapt sports to make them more suitable for children (see pages 37 to 42 for further information).

Stage 3: Performing

- Children react more slowly than adults – give them as little as possible to think about and as much time as possible in which to think about it.

- When coaching beginners, start by making most decisions for them. Explain why the decision was made and encourage them to think for themselves next time.

- Plan practice sessions which offer only limited choices, with enough time for children to choose and use the necessary skill. The smaller the group, the easier it is for them to make decisions.

- As children improve, change the speed and the available space to make each task more difficult.

- To keep children interested, tell them what you are doing and discuss with them what to do next.

21

Figure 2: The stages of skill development

Positive feedback – a vital link

Many participants find it hard to assess their own performance. Children find it especially difficult because they have so much less experience. You can help them a lot by telling them when they are doing well and by making it easy for them to tell you when they encounter difficulties. Communication is the key – if they are having problems, ask them to look at one, or at most, two aspects of the skill at a time and then talk with them about their performance. For children this feedback is a vital link – some of them will find it very hard to improve without your active help.

Skill teaching

In general, there are two approaches to teaching skills:

• Shaping

• Chaining.

Shaping involves accepting a less than ideal version of the skill at first. To begin with, parts of the skill are left out and then added later as the children

master basic skills. The idea is to gradually shape a child's performance by developing strengths, improving weaknesses and adding new refinements.

Chaining involves breaking the action down into a series of simple steps. Children can then practise each step until they are competent at it, before moving on to the next. Two or more steps can be practised together once the child is ready. Eventually the child will learn all the steps necessary for the complete action.

The choice between shaping and chaining depends on the skill you are teaching. Everyone, including children, finds big movements easier to learn than small, accurate movements. To begin with, shaping may be the right choice. If the movement is simple it is best to teach it as a complete unit. Complex movements with many subsidiary parts, such as the long jump, are best taught in a chain. Try to make each part of the chain a meaningful exercise in itself and remember some children may have more difficulty than others with particular parts of the chain. Chaining may not be appropriate, however, for a complex movement in which timing is critical, such as breaststroke.

Teach skills in a sensible sequence – start at a simple level and move on to more difficult levels. Be patient with the children: recognise their limitations and try to see difficulties from their point of view. Children have a short attention span so avoid long, boring practice sessions. For young children, break up practice sessions into units dealing with different skills or aspects of a particular skill. Children enjoy using what they have learned, so give them a chance to use their new skills as quickly as possible.

Where next?

For further information about developing skill, refer to **sports coach UK**'s resource[1] *Improving Practices and Skill.*

Practical tips

- Treat each child as an individual.
- Make sure they are ready to learn – emotionally as well as physically.
- Explain what you want, demonstrate it and give them plenty of time to try out the skill.
- Keep practice fun, varied and active.
- Let them use their skills in a meaningful situation as soon as they are ready.
- Correct mistakes one at a time.
- Start with big, simple movements; develop basic movement patterns before you try to teach specialist skills.
- Guide children's attention to the most important things.
- Make sure you get on the children's wavelength – listen to them and talk to them in their language and at their level.
- Be positive – encourage rather than criticise them.

23

---

1   Available from **Coachwise 1st4sport** (tel 0113-201 5555 or visit www.1st4sport.com).

The mind of a child

Adults often assume that sport helps children to learn to work together and to develop positive attitudes to fair play. This may be true but remember children may see sport quite differently – as just another kind of play, and a means of social contact with their friends. They soon find that sport also involves competition with other children – while some will succeed, many others will fail.

Some children react badly to the competitive element in sport. If they don't do well, their self-esteem is threatened and they feel under stress. Some people therefore argue that competition is harmful to children and makes them drop out of sport. However, in itself, competition is neither good nor bad – it all depends on the attitudes and personal skills of the adult leadership. You are in a unique position to create a positive atmosphere where effort and progress are just as important as winning. If you can achieve that, sport will be a positive experience for every child.

How children see themselves

As they grow up, children are learning about the world around them all the time. They are also developing an image of themselves shaped by:

- the aims they have for themselves

- their achievements in competition

- other children's achievements

- feedback from adults.

Very small children think of themselves as the centre of the world but once they reach school age, children pay much more attention to other people. This is mostly because they have very little experience on which to base judgements of their own. Even so, they find it hard to discriminate between what adults say and what other children tell them, while some independent children still tend to rely on their own judgement. Adolescents become better at self-judgement, balancing what others say with their own assessments. In those growing years, the influence of other people can be very powerful.

The ring of influence

Every child is surrounded by a *ring of influence* that may include peer groups, parents/carers, teachers, youth leaders and you, the coach. Such influential people are sometimes called *significant others* and their behaviour can help to shape the child's self-image. This may be a positive or a negative influence and can induce stress.

The child looks to all these people for help, encouragement and support. Children are easily led, anxious to please and prone to over-enthusiasm. As a coach, you can play a vital part in ensuring that the child's interests are put first.

Children usually begin cooperative play[1] around the age of five. After that, friendship becomes increasingly important to them. At nine or so they may well belong to a small, tight-knit group already competing to see *who's best* at any number of activities. From then on, friends are a major influence and may persuade some children to try sports they would never attempt on their own. Cooperation and teamwork are better at this age, but children are also much more aware of their own skills and those of their peers.

actionplus

25

---

1   Play that involves communication, interaction and cooperation with others.

During adolescence, peer groups can become the dominant influence, sometimes conflicting with parents/carers and authority. Teenagers often adopt the values of the group in preference to adult values and judge themselves by whether their friends approve of what they do. This is not altogether a bad thing – groups often develop a powerful *team spirit* and they learn to use each other's strengths in a positive way.

You can open new doors to young people and give them new standards for self-judgement. By providing regular positive feedback you can show them strengths they never knew they had and build up their confidence. Your encouragement and support will help them to trust their own judgement instead of doing what other children think they should do. You may not replace the influence of the peer group but you can certainly balance it.

Children first, winning second

This is vital if children are to find sport a positive experience. Too often, losing is regarded as failure and winning as success. This means that far more children will be classed as failures than as succeeders and negative experiences could outnumber positive ones.

What is more, if you over-emphasise outcome rather than performance, you are likely to raise the level of competitive stress – the young participants worry about failing and become concerned that those around them will think badly of them. This fear of failure and its consequences has been shown to be the major reason why children drop out of competitive sport.

Sport should be fun. If children don't enjoy it you will achieve nothing at all – except perhaps, to produce adults who will neither play sport themselves nor encourage their own children to do so. The more fun sport is, the less stressful it will be.

Setting goals

You can help children to set goals based on performance (how well they do) rather than on outcome (whether they win or not). In this way, success can be measured in terms of effort, improvement and personal bests – not just victory. These are all achievements over which children have some control and to concentrate on them will help reinforce their self-motivation. This builds positive attitudes towards competition and sport.

Most children's coaches would agree that they aim for all-round development including:

- physical development, using healthy, enjoyable exercise

- skill development – helping children improve performance levels in their chosen sport

- social development, using team games, cooperative skills and fair play

- mental development – establishing and reinforcing confidence.

All these goals can be achieved with a positive approach. Use praise and encouragement, not insults and humiliation, to motivate the children. Show fair play in practice by treating them all with equal consideration. Treat each child as an individual. Don't push elite performers too hard or neglect less gifted children. Given time, slow developers may become star performers. Finally, remember that sport is not the only interest children will have and for some it will not be the most important. Don't ask too much of them in either energy or time. Children need other interests and a good coach puts the child first.

Where next?

For further information about goal-setting, refer to **sports coach UK**'s resources *A Guide to Planning Coaching Programmes* and *Coaching Sessions: a guide to planning and goal-setting*[1].

the mind of a child

27

Liaise with parents/carers

In your coaching you will work with parents/carers, teachers, sports officials and spectators. Encourage them to share your aims and values and to support what you are doing with the children.

Try to establish a good communication system with parents/carers as soon as possible. At the very least, introduce yourself to them at the first coaching session, however busy you are. Better still, consider holding an initial session just for them so you can explain:

- your aims for the season
- your timetable for training/competitions and arrangements for dropping off and picking up
- you may need help with transport
- costs for training and competitions
- kit or equipment required.

This will also provide an opportunity for parents/carers to ask questions and alleviate any concerns they may have.

You are in a position of trust with children and parents/carers will want to be assured that their children will be safe with you.

Liaise with teachers

If you are working with children who are training and competing at a high level (eg in early specialisation sports like gymnastics and diving), you are strongly advised to contact their teachers, possibly via their parents/carers. Make teachers aware of the time and physical/mental pressures faced by the children as a result of their sporting experience. They are likely to be able to make alterations to timetable and homework arrangements, and provide extra support for any lessons that may be missed. Liaising with teachers will also help you to identify periods when the children's participation in training and competitions may need to be reduced to accommodate academic pressures such as SATs and GSCEs.

Practical tips

- Put the child's needs first, winning second.

- Maintain an element of fun during practice sessions and competitions.

- Treat each child as an individual.

- Don't ignore children who need help. If they need support, it is up to you to give it.

- Work with parents/carers, not against them.

- Reinforce attitudes of fair play.

Practical coaching

Having decided on general principles, how can they be put into practice? What allowances should be made for the age and physical development of the children concerned?

Very young children learn through play. By playing with balls and other toys, they learn basic skills that they will use throughout their lives. As they have no experience to use as a yardstick, young children rely on people like you to tell them how well they are doing.

• Keep it fun – let them learn by playing.

• Keep it simple – teach step by step, don't just tell them what to do.

• Praise every small advance, don't criticise. If children are doing something wrong, show them how to do it properly.

Age 6–9

At this age, children are learning to distinguish cause and effect in what they do. However, they still find it hard to separate ability and effort. They tend to think that success depends only on how hard they

try to do something. Be careful how you encourage these children. Telling them they will do better if they try harder may be a mistake, especially if they have little natural ability for what they are trying to do.

• Be patient. Tackle new tasks one at a time and step by step. Let the children learn what you are showing them in their own time.

• Be encouraging. The children are still relying heavily on your judgement. Praise effort as well as achievement.

• Let them explore their limits but don't push them beyond their natural abilities.

• Be accepting. Help minimise the children's fear of failure as they try new activities.

Praise is not the only reward to which children will respond. Play on their natural inquisitiveness, anticipation of reaching a desired goal, involvement with the group or the simple enjoyment of taking part.

Age 10–13

At this age, children are beginning to judge themselves as well as accepting the judgements of others. Even so, up to about the age of 12 they still tend to believe that trying harder can overcome lack of ability. If they do discover their shortcomings, they may find them hard to accept. They will need understanding and support if they are to continue playing sport. Remember that you cannot drive children to do something they don't want to do. It is self-motivation that makes a true performer. You can encourage it but you cannot create it out of nothing.

Some independent children take self-evaluation a step too far. If the standards they set themselves are too high, then no achievements will be good enough.

- Be supportive – help children to accept their natural limits and work within them.

- Be sensitive – encourage children to set realistic goals.

31

Keep it positive

With children, behaviour and discipline must be handled in much the same way as skills training – positively.

- Look for things to praise, particularly in children who might not otherwise gain attention.

- Beginners need plenty of praise. However, once they have developed their skills, praise will be more effective if used selectively.

- Praise good behaviour quickly to show you value it.

- Praise effort and performance more than results. A good shot at goal is still good even if the goalkeeper saves it.

- Don't hold back praise for good play even if it is followed by a mistake.

- Don't mix praise and criticism. 'Great shot, but ...' is not encouraging.

Mistakes will happen

Handling mistakes in a positive way may seem more difficult but it can, and should, be done. In fact, mistakes can be a useful part of learning – if you never make mistakes, you will never learn.

- Remember, participants don't mean to make mistakes. Give encouragement right away and help them to learn from their mistakes.

- Accept mistakes as a necessary part of learning.

- Don't use hostility, sarcasm or shout at the children. It sets a very bad example as well as humiliating and discouraging them.

sports coach UK

Dealing with bad behaviour

Remember you are a role model – perhaps even a hero – for the children you coach. Make sure you yourself practise the behaviour you expect from them and handle their misbehaviour positively.

- Give children a clear idea of the behaviour you expect and follow it yourself.

- Involve the children in making the rules – they are more likely to follow them, and to disapprove of rule-breakers.

- Use time out of practice as a penalty[1] – extra activity should be a reward.

- Don't nag. Give rule-breakers one warning and then a penalty. Children like clear guidelines and firm control.

- One penalty is enough – do it and forget it.

- Be consistent and be fair. Don't favour star performers.

- Reward good behaviour.

Emotions, tears and tantrums

Children get tired and grumpy just like adults. During puberty they may experience emotional difficulties. The pressure of competition can make these even worse, which is another good reason for minimising it. Hormonal changes in boys and girls can produce emotional reactions on their own but there can also be more obvious triggers such as shyness, conflict with parents/carers, relationship problems, money worries and fears about schoolwork. Take these problems seriously; expect emotional outbursts and be caring in your response.

Developing teamwork

Children's social life becomes more and more complex as they grow up. As well as meeting new people, they are also discovering new ways of relating to them. Teamwork in particular involves a set of relationships too complex for young children to grasp. Children playing football tend to form a milling mass around

33

---

1   In this context, the term *penalty* means a form of punishment

the ball – they are all playing as individuals. To play a team game, children must understand the rules and their tasks as members of the team. They must also understand the tasks of all the other team members. To help them you can:

- keep the teams small

- swap players from one position to another

- simplify the rules.

Be careful not to swap players between positions too quickly or without proper instruction – this can leave a young player hopelessly confused. It is always advisable to start with smaller groups until skills and roles have been learned.

Having fewer players also reduces the number of choices open to them and thus simplifies decision-making. Children can be baffled by too much choice, so start by limiting their choices. Once they are confident, you can present more difficult situations which offer a larger number of possibilities.

Simplifying the rules is one good way of reducing choices. Remember, rules are normally written for games played at an adult level. Try not to be rigid – think of the rules as a framework that may need to be built up a piece at a time. Introduce rules as they are needed and adapt them in order to focus on what you want the children to learn.

> ### Where next?
> See pages 37 to 42 for further information about adapting sports for children.

Make it fun

Is competition good or bad? Are children naturally competitive or do they learn it from adults? Does competition mean humiliation for the losers? What is a coach supposed to do?

Start by considering the children's age. Young children don't have an adult view of what competition means. In fact some researchers believe that children don't grasp the full meaning of competition until adolescence.

Competition is natural in many sports but by putting achievement before winning you make it just another part of the game – and there is still room for the losers. Not every child reacts badly to losing but success at sport is still often seen as a means of winning social acceptance.

Although competition is an important part of sport, it should not be the major emphasis of any coaching programme. The Long-term Athlete Development (LTAD) model[1] suggests a ratio of 3:1 in favour of practice over competitive games, enabling children to develop the necessary skills to deal with competitive games. And remember that practices can be used to introduce elements of competition.

Too often, pressure from parents/carers and coaches creates an inappropriate competitive environment. If the focus is purely on winning and losing, at least half of the children competing in a team game are set to fail. If you make a child feel like a failure, that child will not want to continue in sport. To avoid this:

- keep competition informal with young children – don't impose adult ideas

- emphasise achievement and reward effort

- encourage those who realise they have less ability

- help all children – many will wish to play for fun rather than to win.

actionplus

35

Practical tips

- Don't pursue winning for its own sake – put children first and winning second.

- Stick to the rules and teach children to do the same, but treat rules as scaffolding to build on, not a restricting cage.

- Encourage teamwork – it will not just happen.

- Work with parents/carers to establish a positive approach to competitive experiences.

- Expect mistakes and use them as a positive step to learning.

- Remember your aim – to help children develop physically, mentally and socially.

Adapt the sport and help the child

Children of the same age can have very different degrees of physical development. Children's physical proportions are changing all the time. Should they be expected to learn adult sports using adult equipment? The answer has to be no. How can you adapt sports to make them more suitable for children?

Rule it out – or change the rules

In theory, differences in physical maturity make contact sports unsuitable for young children. Games like football, which demand frequent contact, are very popular with this age group. The answer is to change the form of the game to minimise or at least control the degree of contact. In sports such as rugby, formalised competitive collision is part of the game. However, it has been recognised that children should develop avoidance skills like swerving, dodging and sprinting before being introduced to tackling, hence the development of tag rugby.

Safety must be your prime consideration – ensure children wear protective clothing or devise a non-contact form of the game. If the Rugby Football Union can change the laws of scrummage to reduce injury, you can change rules too. Boys are not physically ready for collision sports until they reach puberty and girls cannot be fairly matched with boys in any contact sport after puberty.

The same principle can be used in other sports. Keep the essential features of the game but modify the rules so they are suited to the children's current abilities. In this way the children will gain a sense of achievement and satisfaction at each stage of their development.

Think about reducing the playing time too – children are less able to cope with a full-length game.

Competitive structures are commonplace in professional sport but they may not be so suitable for children. The aim is to encourage participation, effort and satisfaction rather than winning. Don't impose competitive structures for adults on children. Junior teams cannot replicate the week-in-week-out clash of Premiership football. Consider how much training professional teams do to prepare for each match and follow the same principle with your junior teams.

Keep your coaching in proportion

A child's constantly changing physique will limit the ability to perform skills. Your coaching must take account of this. Adult training methods are not appropriate for children. Some sports are simply not suitable for young children. Be patient with children and take account of their physical development at all stages of training.

Small can be beautiful

Children are relatively weaker than adults, as well as physically smaller. They cannot throw, kick, jump or sprint as far as adults. Reducing the playing area allows children to develop

adult-style moves and tactics that they can carry forward as they grow – as well as giving them the satisfaction and enjoyment that comes with real, recognisable achievement. The advantages in some sports are clear; mini-volleyball, for instance, combines a smaller court with fewer players. This simplified game is ideal for younger players.

Tools for the job

Thinking small should apply to equipment as well as to teams and playing areas. Bats and rackets which are too big or heavy for children will force them to learn a technique that cannot survive into maturity. They will also find it much harder to develop the basic physical skills they need to use the equipment successfully. Safety is another consideration. Children using equipment that does not match their strength and proportions are much more likely to have an accident or suffer injury.

Luckily, manufacturers are also aware of the problem and are producing scaled-down/adapted equipment for children in many different sports. This includes bats and rackets with proportionally larger striking surfaces and slower/lighter balls, both of which help children to hit the ball more easily.

actionplus

Grouping children

As children of the same year group may be up to four years apart in physical development, putting them all together in practice or competition may be very unfair indeed. In contact and collision sports it may even be dangerous. A better criterion might be height and weight but this can cause problems with skilful late developers. Try to ensure that the outcome of any match is never a foregone conclusion by:

- considering weight and size before age

- using skills tests to match suitable components

- using limited age ranges to minimise inequalities

- letting officials move children to more appropriate groups

- offering a wide choice of sports opportunities

- encouraging parents/carers to help children pick the most appropriate activities.

Keeping groups small gives each child more chances to learn and practise skills. It also makes learning the rules of team games easier and reduces decision-making to a level that young children can handle.

Four and five-a-side football, for example, avoids the usual crush of bodies round the ball and allows children to learn real team skills and understand the fundamental principles of the game.

Practical tips

- Fit the sport to the child, not the child to the sport.
- Get equipment that is the right size for your participants' age group and physical development.
- Adapt the rules to achieve better performance and greater satisfaction.
- Create practice routines that meet the children's needs and abilities, and are not simply watered-down versions of adult routines.
- Use grids and other means of marking out smaller playing areas.

40

actionplus

Table 4: Examples of how to adapt sport for children

Sport	Problem	Adaptation
Changing the equipment		
Basketball	Target too high	Lower the ring and/or use a lighter ball
Hurdling	Hurdles too high for some	Place the hurdles at a height and distance to suit the individual
Tennis	Game too fast – not enough time for decisions	Use a slower ball that doesn't bounce so much
Volleyball	Small children afraid of the hard ball	Use a sponge ball that doesn't hurt when hit
Squash	Racket too long and heavy	Use a shorter, lighter racket that allows the child to learn the right technique – one that will survive into maturity
Netball	Goalpost too high/small	Lower the goalpost and use a larger ring and/or a smaller ball
Changing the playing area		
Lacrosse	Children cannot cover full-size pitch	Play *poplacrosse*, which reduces the playing area according to the number of children and the facility available
Cricket	Child cannot hit to the boundary	Shorten the boundary but keep the wicket full-size

41

Continued ...

Table 4 (continued)

adapt the sport and help the child

Sport	Problem	Adaptation
Changing the rules		
Basketball	Too many rules too soon	Start with a small number of simple rules and gradually introduce more as children become more competent
Rugby	Too many players	Play mini-rugby with 18 or even fewer players
Tennis	Sets too demanding	Use shorter sets, and allow longer breaks in between for full recovery
Volleyball	Difficulty striking the ball as it comes over the net	Allow the ball to bounce once

Legal and ethical responsibilities

As a coach, it is essential that you understand your responsibilities in terms of ethical behaviour and legally acceptable practice.

Child protection

One of the most important legal issues for coaches working with children concerns child protection. Coaches have a responsibility to protect:

- their participants from child abuse

- themselves from wrongful accusations.

The effects of abuse on children can be devastating and can lead to severe problems in childhood and later in life. It is therefore vital that you are aware of the types of child abuse and that you can recognise the signs and respond in the correct manner.

sports coach UK

There are five main kinds of abuse:

- **Neglect** (eg leaving children unsupervised, inadequate food, warmth or clothing).

- **Emotional abuse** (eg persistent lack of love and affection, being threatened or taunted, parents/carers or coaches whose overwhelming ambition for the child exceeds that of the child).

- **Sexual abuse** (eg sexual intercourse, masturbation, being shown pornographic material).

- **Physical abuse** (eg hitting, shaking, being given alcohol or drugs, excessive training regimes, use of performance-enhancing or puberty-delaying drugs).

- **Bullying and harassment** (eg physical assaults, name-calling, sarcasm, racist taunts, threats, gestures, unwanted physical contact, graffiti, stealing or hiding personal items).

43

Practical tips

- If a child discloses evidence of abuse, there are a number of steps you should take:

  - Listen and reassure the child that he was right to tell you.

  - Be honest and explain you will need to tell someone else who will be able to help protect him.

  - Don't take sole responsibility – follow the policies and procedures adopted by your organisation. It will have an officer and a system to deal with such issues.

  - Phone the **NSPCC Child Protection Helpline** (0808-800 5000) or **Childline** (0800-1111) for confidential advice.

  - Accurately record what the child said and what action you have taken.

- If you suspect a child is being abused, there are a number of steps you could take:

  - Talk to the parents/carers to clarify any injury or change in behaviour unless you think this may place the child at further risk.

  - Inform your organisation's Child Protection Officer and follow the child protection policy.

  - Phone the **NSPCC Child Protection Helpline** (0808-800 5000) or **Childline** (0800-1111) for confidential advice.

  - Seek medical attention if required.

It is important for coaches to reduce the risk of wrongful accusation and promote good practice. Here are some guidelines:

- Avoid situations where there is just one adult and one child.

- Keep doors open when working in an enclosed environment.

- Arrange to meet children with parents/carers present.

- Encourage parents/carers and other adults to observe coaching sessions and support competitions.

- Follow your national governing body's guidelines if physical support of a child is required (eg in gymnastics).

Where next?

- Remember – if you are worried about a child and need to talk to someone in confidence, call the **NSPCC Child Protection Helpline** (0808-800 5000) or **Childline** (0800-1 1 1 1).

- For further guidance on child protection issues in coaching, refer to the following **sports coach UK** resources[1]:

  – *Protecting Children: A Guide for Sportspeople* (home study pack)

  – *Safe and Sound* (leaflet)

- For further guidance on child protection issues in sport in general, contact the Child Protection in Sport Unit[2].

---

1 Available from **Coachwise 1st4sport** (tel 0113-201 5555 or visit www.1st4sport.com).

2 See page 50 for contact details.

Legislation

There are now many pieces of legislation that have a direct impact on coaches working with children. These include the:

- Children Act 1999
- Protection of Children Act 1999
- Criminal Justice and Court Services Act 2000.

In April 2001 Sport England made it mandatory for all national governing bodies receiving grant aid to have a child protection policy. It is important that you and/or your club are familiar with, and adhere to, your respective policy. All sports organisations with a child protection policy will have a lead child protection officer who will be able to offer support and guidance.

actionplus

actionplus

actionplus

Where next?

Coaching children is a big responsibility but it can be a very enjoyable one. It is important to remember some simple guidelines.

By taking account of physical and mental changes, you can support children at every stage of development, helping them to reach their personal peak of fitness and skill. By putting children first and thinking positively, you can bring satisfaction and achievement into their lives. By actively working with other adults you can create the right environment for continuing enjoyment. By putting effort, progress and team spirit before winning, you can encourage discipline, fair-mindedness and sporting behaviour. By adapting rules and equipment to suit children's needs, you can create more realistic goals for them to achieve. If you can practise all of these qualities, you will introduce children to a new world of exciting possibilities.

sports coach UK (scUK) offers a variety of workshops and resources related to coaching children and young people.

Workshops

*   Coaching Children and Young People
*   Good Practice and Child Protection

For more information about these workshops, contact your nearest Regional Training Unit (RTU). RTU contact details are available from **scUK** (tel 0113-274 4802 or visit www.sportscoachuk.org).

Resources

The following resources are available from **Coachwise 1st4sport** (tel 0113-201 5555 or visit www.1st4sport.com):

* Campbell, S and Crisfield, P (1997) **Making sport fun**. Leeds, National Coaching Foundation.
ISBN 0 947850 56 2

* Crouch, M and Lester, G et al (2002) **Protecting children: a guide for sportspeople**. 3rd edition. Leeds, Coachwise Solutions.
ISBN 0 947850 50 3

* Hagger, M (1999) **Coaching young performers**. Leeds, National Coaching Foundation.
ISBN 1 902523 15 6

* **sports coach UK** (2001) **Code of conduct for sports coaches**. Leeds, Coachwise Solutions.

* **sports coach UK** (updated 2001) **Safe and sound** (leaflet). Leeds, Coachwise Solutions.

The following resource is available from **scUK** (tel 0113-274 4802):

* **sports coach UK** (updated 2002) **Child protection – policy and implementation procedures**. Leeds, **sports coach UK**.

Other resources in the Coaching Essentials[1] series include:

How to Coach Disabled People in Sport

This resource tackles all the frequently asked questions posed by sports teachers, coaches and participants about how to work with disabled sportspeople. As well as a whole spectrum of new ideas for inclusion, the resource will introduce and offer guidance to any coach involved with disabled people in sport. (Based on *Working With Disabled Sportspeople*.)

---

1   Available from **Coachwise 1st4sport** (tel 0113-201 5555 or visit www.1st4sport.com).

How to Coach Sports Safely

Focusing on safe practice in sport, this resource outlines the health and safety issues associated with coaching. Includes new sections on managing risk and manual handling. Essential guidance for every coach. (Based on *Safety and Injury*.)

How to Coach Sports Effectively

This resource includes practical tips to help develop coaching skills and allow participants to get the most benefits from your sessions. Also features chapters on planning, organising and delivering sessions. Everything you need to be an effective coach. (Based on *Planning and Practice*.)

What is Sports Coaching?

This new resource clearly defines coaching and introduces the basic components of coaching sessions. Including sections on the roles, responsibilities and qualities of a coach, it is an ideal resource for new and existing coaches. (Based on *The Coach In Action*.)

Useful contacts

sports coach UK

sports coach UK (scUK) works closely with national governing bodies to provide a comprehensive service for coaches throughout the UK. This includes an extensive programme of workshops which have proved valuable to coaches from all types of sport and every level of experience. For details of **scUK** workshops in your area, contact your nearest Regional Training Unit. For more information about **scUK**'s workshops and other services, contact:

sports coach UK
114 Cardigan Road
Headingley
Leeds LS6 3BJ
Tel: 0113-274 4802
Fax: 0113-275 5019

E-mail
coaching@sportscoachuk.org
Website
www.sportscoachuk.org

where next?

49

British Sports Trust

The British Sports Trust is responsible for the organisation of the Sports Leader Awards:

* Junior Sports Leader Award
* Community Sports Leader Award
* Higher Sports Leader Award
* Basic Expedition Leader Award.

These are training courses run by schools and community groups, designed to increase the confidence and organisational and delivery skills of people wishing to run physical activities.

British Sports Trust
Clyde House
10 Milburn Avenue
Oldbrook
Milton Keynes
MK6 2WA
Tel: 01908-689180

E-mail
admin@bst.org.uk
Website
www.bst.org.uk

Child Protection in Sport Unit

Established in 2000 by Sport England in partnership with the NSPCC, the Child Protection in Sport Unit (CPSU) coordinates and oversees the development of child protection across sport.

Child Protection in Sport Unit
NSPCC National Training Centre
3 Gilmour Close
Beaumont Leys
Leicester
LE4 1EZ
Tel: 0116-234 7278/7280
Fax: 0116-234 0464

E-mail
cpsu@nspcc.org.uk
Website
www.sportprotects.org.uk

National governing bodies

The national governing body for your sport or activity will give advice on coaching courses and other relevant information. National governing body contact details are available from:

> **Central Council of Physical Recreation (CCPR)**
> Francis House
> Francis Street
> London
> SW1P 1DE
> Tel: 020-7854 8500
> Fax: 020-7854 8501
>
> **E-mail**
> info@ccpr.org.uk
> **Website**
> www.ccpr.org.uk

Youth Sport Trust

The Youth Sport Trust (YST) works in close partnership with schools and sport to provide quality physical education and sport programmes for young people aged 18 months to 18 years. The YST TOPs programme provides a series of linked and progressive schemes for young people, and delivers training and adapted equipment for teachers, coaches and sports leaders.

> **Youth Sport Trust**
> Beckwith Centre for Sport
> Loughborough University
> Loughborough
> LE11 3TU
> Tel: 01509-228293
> Fax: 01509-210851
>
> **Website**
> www.youthsport.net/yst